ROLLING STONES

A Retrospective • 1962-2012

Michael Heatley

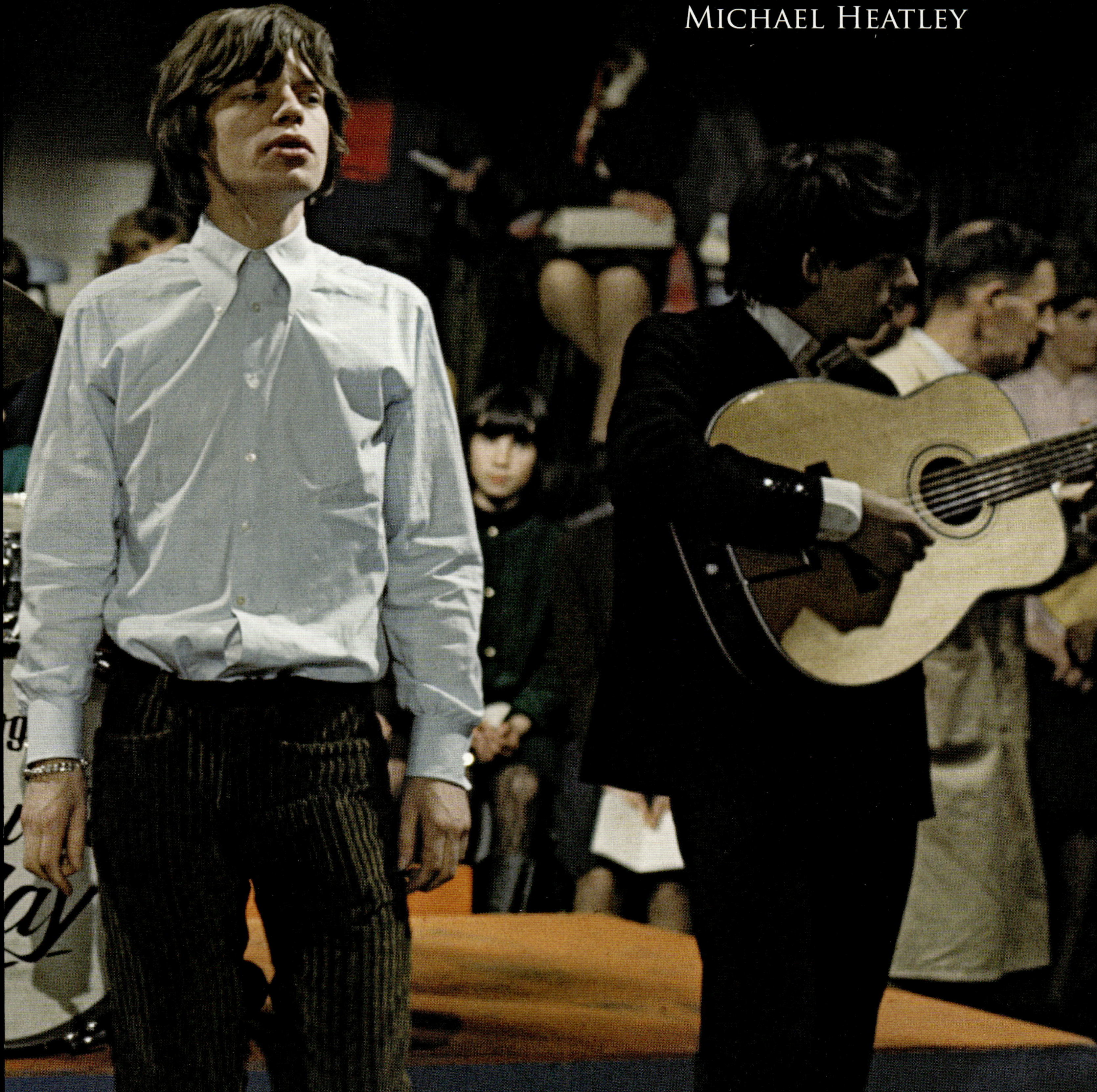

THE AUTHOR

Michael Heatley is the author of
over one hundred biographies, as
well as editor of reference books on
sport, popular and classical music.
He has written for *Radio Times* and
the *Mail On Sunday*.

Published by: Wilkinson Publishing Pty Ltd ACN 006 042 173
Level 4, 2 Collins Street Melbourne, Victoria,
Australia 3000 Ph: +61 3 9654 5446
www.wilkinsonpublishing.com.au
International distribution by Pineapple Media Limited
(www.pineapple-media.com) ISSN: 1839 – 1737
ISBN 978-1-921804-66-3 CiP pending.

Not Fade Away
Why the Stones still matter after a half-century in the spotlight

The Rolling Stones are more than just a band. Not only did they write and perform great songs, they were also at the forefront of a movement in the Sixties that believed music could change the world. But the Stones' brand of revolution was confrontational, to say the least.

While flower-power bands preached peace and love, these raunchy rockers were down and dirty, pulling no lyrical punches as to what they were after (satisfaction) and how they intended to get it (spending the night together). They weren't averse to a bit of street fighting, either …

The teenager had been invented in the Fifties, the era of Elvis, and the Stones kicked the youth revolution up a notch or two. Only Bill Wyman was old enough to have done two years' compulsory national service in the UK armed forces, but things like this and food and clothing rationing were all too recent reminders of the cold, grey war years. Life was different now and, though there were still wars in faraway places like Vietnam, the battle was now between youth and the establishment. And, to their millions of fans, the Stones were standard-bearers.

From the front of the stage Mick Jagger and Keith Richards have seen the impact made by the Greatest Rock'n'Roll Band in the World at first hand. Mick may now be a Knight of the Realm, but in 1967 he and Keith both heard the cell doors clang behind them as they faced trial on drugs charges. It's been a long, strange trip and, with the ever-reliable Charlie Watts behind them, they've chronicled every step of it in words and music.

So is the show finally over? Will they ever play together again? This is a question only Jagger and Richards, the self-styled 'Glimmer Twins', can answer. But one thing is for certain. The songs they wrote and performed will be heard at discos, danced to at parties, covered by bar bands and enjoyed by millions of fans worldwide for as long as music is played.

The page is too short to list bands like Guns N' Roses, Primal Scream and the Black Crowes who have lifted from the Stones' songbook. But it's the background against which their breakthrough was achieved that sets them apart – an era where adults ruled the roost and teenagers were barely tolerated. "My parents were extremely disapproving of it all," Jagger later recalled, "because it was

just not done. This was for very low-class people ... rock'n'roll singers weren't educated people."

The ever-knowledgeable frontman also knows it's important to remain current. "People have this obsession. They want you to be like you were in 1969 ... because otherwise their youth goes with you. It's very selfish, but it's understandable." That's why the Stones have continued to make records, even if the stage set has remained a mixture of the tried and the trusted. It's a necessary compromise

because Jagger, still the savvy business student, knows that now the battle is won when the public must be satisfied.

At the time of writing he is shaking his tail feather alongside Dave Stewart and Joss Stone in Superheavy, but with all due respect it won't be this 'supergroup' that's remembered after another half-century has passed. It's the Rolling Stones – and the music and impact they made will surely 'Not Fade Away'.

Ladies and gentlemen,
the Rolling Stones

When the Rolling Stones played their first public gig at London's Marquee Club in July 1962, only Mick Jagger and Keith Richards of the 'classic' line-up were actually present, along with guitarist and original leader Brian Jones. Dick Taylor, Ian Stewart and future Kink Mick Avory made up the numbers on bass, piano and drums respectively as the band filled in for regulars Blues Incorporated, who were busy playing a radio session.

The club's patrons were interested in hearing 'authentic blues', but when, a few short months later, female pop fans outside the Marquee's hallowed portals caught sight of the dynamic Jagger shaking his maracas (and a lot else besides), they went wild. The males in the audience could marvel at the cool guitar-slinging of the wild-eyed Richards and the flamboyant Jones, while bassist Bill Wyman and drummer Charlie Watts simply watched impassively.

Wyman and Watts were yet to join when the Rolling Stones made their Marquee bow – but when they did, the band found they'd stumbled on the formula for success. The Stones soon became the biggest draw on the London gig circuit at venues like Studio 51 or the Crawdaddy in Richmond, where they had a residency. The material they played was crowd-pleasing American soul and R&B like Marvin Gaye's *Can I Get A Witness* and *Route 66*, the arrangement stolen from rock'n'roll godfather Chuck Berry.

The Beatles were fascinated by this challenge to their crown and ventured south to meet the newcomers. As a result, John Lennon and Paul McCartney gifted them the previously unrecorded *I Wanna Be Your Man*, a song that would be the Stones' second single. In one critic's words, "Mick Jagger turned the lyrics ... into what could have been a prelude to sexual assault," the Moptops admitting defeat when their later version, an album track, saw drummer Ringo Starr offering a puppydog vocal. No contest!

The Stones had released two more singles, covers of Chuck Berry's *Come On* and Buddy Holly's *Not Fade Away*, when their first album was released in April 1964. As with so many debut discs of the era, it immortalised their stage act, and was recorded 'as-live' on a two-track tape machine with one or two overdubs added. And such was their popularity that, even though none of the singles were included, 'The Rolling Stones' took just eight days to top the UK LP chart thanks to 100,000 advance orders.

The year of 1964 had started well when the Stones appeared on the first ever edition of the BBC's *Top Of The Pops*, broadcast from Manchester. Two UK tours would follow in successive months, with the audience reaction fast going off the scale. The press, who'd invented Beatlemania, happily branded the scruffy, long-haired quintet the Fab Four's parent-unfriendly alternative: headlines like 'Would you let your daughter marry a Rolling Stone?' ensured they sold out everywhere they went. Manager Andrew Oldham, who actually fed the press that particular line, stoked the flames of controversy with relish and encouraged the band to show their wild side.

When the Stones went to the States, they caused a furore on *The Ed Sullivan Show* (which promptly banned all rock'n'roll acts) similar to Elvis a decade earlier. Their notoriety was such that, like their UK debut, their Rolling Stones No 2 album didn't even carry their name on its cover – the forbidding portrait photo was enough. And when that second album followed singles *It's All Over Now* and *Little Red Rooster*, which shot to #1 in the UK charts in early 1965, it was clear the Stones were here to stay.

Albums were all well and good, but it was the singles that spelled out rebellion – *(I Can't Get No) Satisfaction*, their first American #1, *Get Off Of My Cloud* and *Let's Spend The Night Together*, its lyric amended to *Let's spend some time together* to satisfy the censor on US television, all made an immediate and lasting impact. These were no longer cover versions but songs Mick and Keith had created themselves, and were tailor-made to irritate the powers that be.

Somehow the Stones held a mirror to society's seamier side – and the establishment did not like it. A collision course was set, a flashpoint sooner or later certain. Meanwhile, the same 1966 summer that saw England win the football World Cup, saw the release of *Aftermath*, the first Stones album entirely penned by Jagger and Richards; it would spend eight weeks at #1 in Britain, with the subsequent single *Paint It, Black* following it to the top.

"People love talking about when they were young and heard *Honky Tonk Women* for the first time. It's quite a heavy load to carry on your shoulders, the memories of so many people."
Mick Jagger

The year of 1967 was the fabled Summer of Love. The Beatles were busy creating their blissed-out masterpiece in *Sgt Pepper's* – but for the Stones it was one hassle after another. Having sued the *News Of The World* newspaper over what they claimed was false reporting, Keith and Mick were charged with drug offences after Redlands, Keith's country house in Sussex, was raided. The clear inference was that the paper had tipped off the police.

Jagger and Richards spent a night apiece in jail before receiving bail and, eventually, a conditional discharge/acquittal after establishment paper *The Times* unexpectedly came out in their defence. September saw the Stones finally part company with manager Andrew Oldham, while Brian Jones was sentenced to nine months' imprisonment on drugs charges in October; this was later rescinded. Musically, the Stones unusually found themselves followers rather than leaders, *Their Satanic Majesties Request* being compared unfavourably but fairly to *Sgt Pepper*.

After the debacle of Satanic Majesties, *Beggars Banquet* was a special album that in Keith's words "got the essence of the Stones down on tape". American producer Jimmy Miller added a new edge to the sound that was apparent from the moment the music kicked off with the chilling *Sympathy For The Devil*. It would be the last album Brian Jones appeared on as a full member, and he was barely in evidence. His behaviour was now deemed too erratic and he was let go in 1969 – a body blow for the man who founded the band.

Brian's tragic death failed to derail the Stones, who played London's Hyde Park two days later with young replacement Mick Taylor, recruited from John Mayall's Bluesbreakers. They dedicated the day to Brian, as *Honky Tonk Women* headed for the top – their eighth and final UK #1 single preceding the classic *Let It Bleed* album. But the band's sixth US tour hit the buffers at the Altamont speedway track, where a fan was stabbed and killed by an intoxicated member of the Hell's Angels, who were acting as event security. Thus, a wild decade ended on a depressing note.

Mick Jagger, who had dated Chrissie Shrimpton for three years in 1966 before falling for singer Marianne Faithfull, fathered children with soul singer Marsha Hunt and Nicaraguan beauty Bianca De Macias. He married Bianca in St Tropez in 1971.

> "I came into music just because I wanted the bread. It's true. I looked around and this seemed like the only way I was going to get the kind of bread I wanted."
>
> Mick Jagger

"Good music comes out of people playing together, knowing what they want to do and going for it. You have to sweat over it and bug it to death. You can't do it by pushing buttons and watching a TV screen."
Keith Richards

After buying time with the live *Get Yer Ya Ya's Out*, the Stones hit the Seventies running. *Sticky Fingers* (1971) was a classic, from its Andy Warhol 'zipper' cover to the music it contained, and was the first on the band's own Rolling Stones Records label with its famous 'lips' logo. They then fled to France for tax reasons, but chose to live separately, the geographical separation making it harder to make records. But *Exile On Main Street* more than repaid the six months it took to make (not to mention a similar time to mix), the double album backing up Keith's opinion that his drug habits "didn't affect my productivity at all".

Though it topped both UK and US charts, many fans who bought *Exile* hated its low-fi sound and muddy mix. All the plaudits it has picked up have been in contemporary times as other bands have emulated the sleazy, after-hours ambience; according to engineer Andy Johns, "no-one would plug anything in until midnight". The Stones were once again ahead of the game, and a reissue of the album in 2010, complete with previously discarded tracks, received worldwide critical acclaim.

In 1975 Mick Taylor quit the Stones after five and a half years. "My attitude towards the other four members is one of respect ... but now is the time to move on and do something new," he said. Veteran Ron Wood, a great friend of Keith's, was named as fifth Stone for the summer tour, technically on loan from Rod Stewart's Faces, but he would not return to Rod the Mod's side.

Mick Jagger met blonde Texan fashion model Jerry Hall, with whom he would have four children, in 1977. She was the fiancé of Bryan Ferry, but swiftly changed rock-star horses. They eventually married in 1990 but this was annulled in 1999, ending 22 years together.

The Seventies brought a studio album every two years, the highlight being 1978's *Some Girls* and disco-styled single *Miss You.* Both topped their respective US chart as the band headed off on a ninth Stateside tour. Punk was the coming thing at home, but Keith's brushes with the law in Canada and Ronnie's alleged friendship with the Prime Minister's wife (Margaret Trudeau) reminded observers that the Stones were the original rock'n'roll rebels.

Emotional Rescue carried on where *Some Girls* left off in 1980, but the songs were denied the chance to grow on stage when Jagger decided he didn't want to tour. His availability was limited by his burgeoning film career which had him up a creek (literally) in Peru filming *Fitzcarraldo*. And the wedge this drove between himself and Keith would render this something of a lost decade for the Stones, though they did celebrate their 20th anniversary as a band with their first European tour in six years.

Keith Richards' long-term girlfriend had been Italian-born actress Anita Pallenberg, who entered the Stones circle as girlfriend of

"Taking drugs on a recreational level
is one thing. But taking them
while you're working on a stage is,
you know, I don't think it was that great."
Mick Jagger

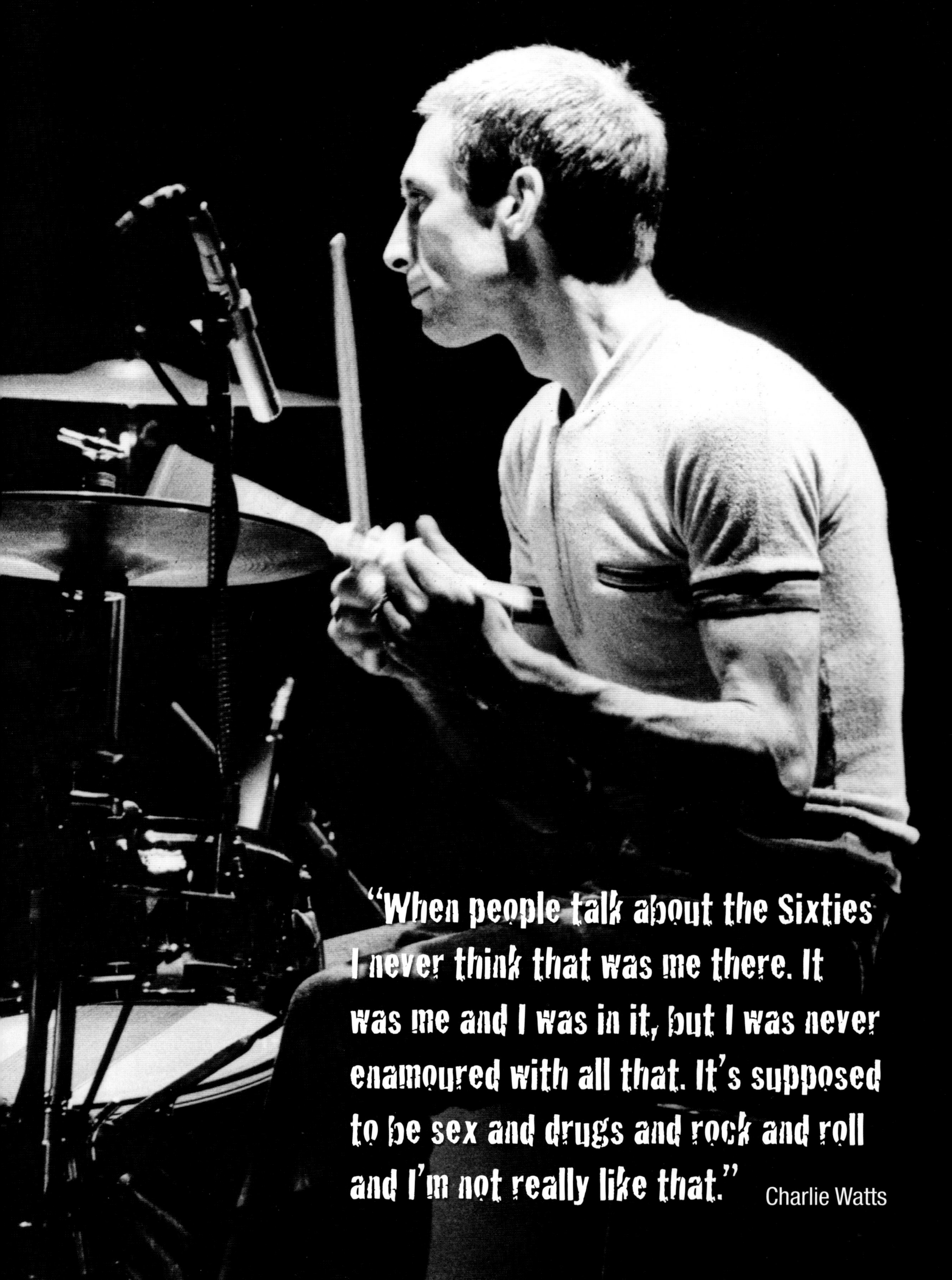"When people talk about the Sixties I never think that was me there. It was me and I was in it, but I was never enamoured with all that. It's supposed to be sex and drugs and rock and roll and I'm not really like that."
Charlie Watts

Brian Jones. They stayed together until 1979 and had three children: son Marlon, daughter Angela (originally named Dandelion) and another boy, Tara, who died less than three months after his birth.

Later in 1979, Richards met model Patti Hansen, a model for Calvin Klein and Revlon. Richards and Hansen married in December 1983 on Keith's 40th birthday in Cabo San Lucas, the ceremony filmed by Julien Temple. The couple have two daughters, Theodora and Alexandra.

Jagger was left alone in the studio by Keith to mix 1983's *Undercover*, fuelling rumours of a rift. *Dirty Work* (1987) saw the situation reversed; Mick was involved with his solo work, so this was a Keith Richards record. But it was no *Exile*; twenty session musicians were employed to record the least Stones-like Stones album ever. And when they finished the record, Mick suddenly decided not to tour, signalling the biggest fall-out ever between the songwriting duo. The damage, fuelled by a public slanging match, would take time and work to repair.

By 1989 the hatchet had been buried between the 'Glimmer Twins', who were both present in January when the Stones were inducted into the Rock and Roll Hall of Fame. Though Charlie and Bill elected not to attend, Mick Taylor celebrated the recognition with Mick, Keith and Ron. In March they contracted to play fifty North American dates on the Steel Wheels Tour, their first for seven years, kicking off in Philadelphia in August.

By 1993, Bill Wyman was an ex-Stone: "I thought the last two tours were the best we have ever done, so I was quite happy to stop." He was replaced on 1994's *Voodoo Lounge* – the band's first UK chart-topper since *Emotional Rescue* – by ex-Miles Davis bassist Darryl Jones, who remains with the band today.

The Unplugged vogue encouraged by *MTV* finally ensnared the Stones in 1995. The suitably titled *Stripped* was recorded in 1995, and ventured outside the usual repertoire, including some blues classics among the self-penned songs.

September 2002 saw the band heading off on a world tour that opened in Boston's Fleet Center and extended through 2003. It was intended to promote *Forty Licks*, a greatest hits double album released to mark forty years as a band.

On 26 July 2005, Jagger's 62nd birthday, the band announced *A Bigger Bang*, their first album of new material in almost eight years; this made the transatlantic Top 3. The worldwide tour promoting it between August 2005 and August 2007 was the second highest-grossing of all time; only U2 could better the $558,255,524 earned. The final show in the O2 in London on 26 August 2007 is the last concert the Stones would play – and with relations between Mick and Keith at another low following the latter's controversial autobiography,

it's impossible to say if, when and where the next one will take place.

It had been a long, strange trip from the Marquee Club in central London back in 1962, to the O2 just a few miles across town in Greenwich. They'd played shows across the world in clubs, arenas, sports stadia, the Copacabana beach in Rio and even on the Internet; a 1994 show was streamed online as an early example of this new technology. If the O2 show really was 'The Last Time', the Stones have bowed out in style.

Just don't bet your house on it …

Love You Live
On stage, the Stones are in a league of their own.
We chart their highpoints.

Live performance has always been the lifeblood of the Rolling Stones. Never at their happiest in the studio, it was when grinding out their trademark riffs to an appreciative audience that they really came alive.

Their first opportunity to do just that came at London's Marquee Club in July 1962. With resident band Blues Incorporated busy playing a radio session, the embryonic Stones filled their usual slot. The line-up comprised Mick, Keith, Brian, bassist Dick Taylor, pianist Ian Stewart and future Kinks drummer Mick Avory.

Their stage act was further honed at a club in Richmond, West London, called the Crawdaddy, run by young entrepreneur (and, briefly, Stones manager) Giorgio Gomelsky. They moved onwards and upwards at top speed, and by 1964 they were headlining their own tours and topping the bill at the now renamed National Jazz and Blues Festival.

The last week of April 1964 saw the band's first appearance at the prestigious New Musical Express Poll-Winners Concert at the Empire Pool, Wembley just prior to the release of their debut album.

On 1 August 1965 the Stones made their debut at the London Palladium, the Mecca of British light entertainment. The Walker Brothers and the Moody Blues were among the supporting acts. By this time authorities were cracking down on enthusiastic fans: the *New Musical Express* reported "Teenage girls (were) roughly manhandled in the gangways by officials using Gestapo-like methods".

The following month brought their second UK tour that saw the Stones play two sets a night at twenty four theatre venues up and down the country, while the end of October brought their second tour of the

WEM

States; this took them through to Los Angeles in December. Similar tours took place in 1966, albeit at larger venues; the London date was upgraded from the Finsbury Park Astoria to the Royal Albert Hall. An Australian tour was also added in February.

The year of 1969 will be remembered for two Stones concerts in particular: the first, a free festival on 5 July in London's Hyde Park, was to an estimated 250,000 people. The band dedicated the day to Brian Jones, who had died days earlier, and Mick released some white butterflies from the front of the stage to symbolise his sprit soaring free. The second and less auspicious date was five months later at Altamont, of which more later.

Stones gigs and tours in the States were always notable events – and few more so than the 1972 epic that promoted their *Exile On Main Street* album. Opening act Stevie Wonder, on the verge of superstardom, pushed them every step of the way performance-wise.

Knebworth House in Hertfordshire hosted the Stones in 1976, the band following in the footsteps of Pink Floyd who'd played there the previous year. They played a circus-themed outdoor gig to 200,000 fans, and it was one of the longest shows of their career. This was some consolation for the delay they made the punters endure so that the lighting effects could be seen properly in full darkness.

"To make a rock'n'roll record,
technology is the least important thing."

Keith Richards

"The last show we played, I was straight as a die.
It did feel weird not to be hiding behind alcohol or dope,
but being focused was . . . good."

Ron Wood

The following year saw a pair of gigs at the other end of the size scale at Toronto's El Mocambo Club. There the band played to a three-hundred-strong invited audience, including the Prime Minister's wife Margaret Trudeau, at a venue that first opened its doors in 1850. It was their first live club date in fourteen years and they billed themselves as the Cockroaches. When the double album *Love You Live* emerged in September, one vinyl side was dedicated to music from the second show.

The Rolling Stones' European Tour in 1982, to promote the album *Tattoo You*, was a continuation of their 1981 US tour and climaxed with two outdoor dates at London's Wembley Stadium in June. This would be their last tour for seven years.

The Eighties brought much personal strife in the Stones camp, particularly between Mick and Keith. But all were united in grief at the passing of Ian 'Stu' Stewart, their original piano-player and long-time road manager. London's 100 Club, a tiny basement in Oxford Street, was the venue chosen for a tribute gig on 25 February 1986. Two days later the Stones were in Hollywood, where Eric Clapton presented them with a Lifetime Achievement Grammy.

After releasing the critically acclaimed *Steel Wheels* album in 1989, Mick, Keith, Ron, Bill and Charlie made up their collective mind to go back on the road. There'd earlier been an extended – and increasingly ominous – period of silence from the band as Jagger and Richards, the musical marriage whose songs had fuelled the band's success, endured a trial separation. Words had been exchanged in the press, but hatchets were buried and differences forgotten to rekindle the legend.

Next up was the *Voodoo Lounge* tour, whose stage included a 45-foot inflatable Elvis Presley, plus a huge, metal-scaled snake called the Cobra incorporating forty eight aircraft landing lights. Optional extras included twenty one further inflatable characters, among them a 35-foot black friar, a baby's head and a 15-foot goat skull. The set would remain hidden in a Toronto aircraft hangar until the opening concert in Washington in August 1994.

There weren't many places the Stones hadn't played nor landmarks they hadn't reached by 2006, but two gigs that year stand out in particular. The first was in February when they played a special show on Rio De Janeiro's Copacabana Beach to an estimated 1.5 million people – their biggest audience ever.

In April, the Stones performed for the first time ever in mainland China in front of 8,000 fans at Shanghai's Grand Stage. Chinese rock star Cui Jian enjoyed a guest spot with vocals and acoustic guitar on Wild Horses, but censorship by the authorities ensured that *Rough Justice, Honky Tonk Women* and *Brown Sugar* were left off the set list. The Stones first visit to China, scheduled for April 2003, had been called off due to a flu epidemic.

This was all part and parcel of the Bigger Bang tour that, to this date, remains their last. An encore is eagerly demanded, and equally awaited.

"I'd rather be dead than singing Satisfaction when I'm forty-five."

Mick Jagger, 1975

The Glimmer Twins

Mick Jagger and Keith Richards are the childhood friends who wrote the soundtrack for a generation. What makes them tick?

The relationship between Mick Jagger and Keith Richards has always been central to the Rolling Stones' appeal and success. Re-kindled on a railway platform in Dartford in 1960, it has survived many a crisis and produced some great music – even if, like Lennon and McCartney, the songs have not always been (pardon the pun) joint efforts.

The pair couldn't have had more contrasting lifestyles. Jagger has been at pains to retain his physical fitness, an essential prerequisite for a frontman. Indeed, his continuing mastery of the pout and pirouette was noted by US band Maroon 5, who enjoyed a chart-topping single in 2011 with a song entitled *Moves Like Jagger*. To still be leading the field and providing a generation with a role model after half a century is testament to his enduring youth.

The pair's brief imprisonment on drugs charges in 1967 seemed to spur Mick into cleaning up his act – give or take a single lapse. Keith, by contrast, was still being busted for drugs as late as 1978. The various myths surrounding his health included the claim that he had his blood changed once a month, while his rotting teeth and an increasingly ravaged appearance suggested another rock'n'roll casualty in the making. Happily he, too, regained his grip on reality and, apart from falling out of the occasional coconut tree, seems to have retained it.

Musically, the pair have continued to gel. It's always been assumed that Jagger contributed the lyrics and Richards the music, but that is an oversimplification. Certain numbers have been more or less solo efforts (Jagger claims *Brown Sugar* exclusively, for instance), yet there's no doubt that Keith's gritty authenticity and love for the blues has kept Mick's flights of fantasy firmly nailed down.

It was the decision to replace blues covers with self-penned songs, beginning with the 1966 album *Aftermath*, instigated by manager Andrew Oldham, that ensured the Stones would rival the Beatles as the most successful 'self-contained' group of the Sixties.

The Glimmer Twins' stranglehold on the songwriting and, from the Seventies, production, has led to a revolving door in the guitar department. Brian Jones and Mick Taylor were both miffed that their contributions to the music were not reflected in the credits, while bass guitarist Bill Wyman even registered a solo Top 20 hit of his own (*Si Si Je Suis Un Rock Star*) as a pointed 'two fingers' to the musical monopoly that had restricted him for so long. Ron Wood, a close friend of Keith's, accepted the status quo from the outset, though he picked up co-writing credits in the Eighties.

The first major divide between Jagger and Richards happened in the Eighties, a decade in which their touring had been less than continuous. While Live Aid saw the likes of Queen and U2 make a pitch to be recognised as heirs to the title of the World's Greatest Rock'n'Roll Band, Jagger and Richards appeared in solo capacities. Jagger performed solo, abetted by Tina Turner, while Richards recruited Ronnie Wood to flank Bob Dylan with acoustic guitars.

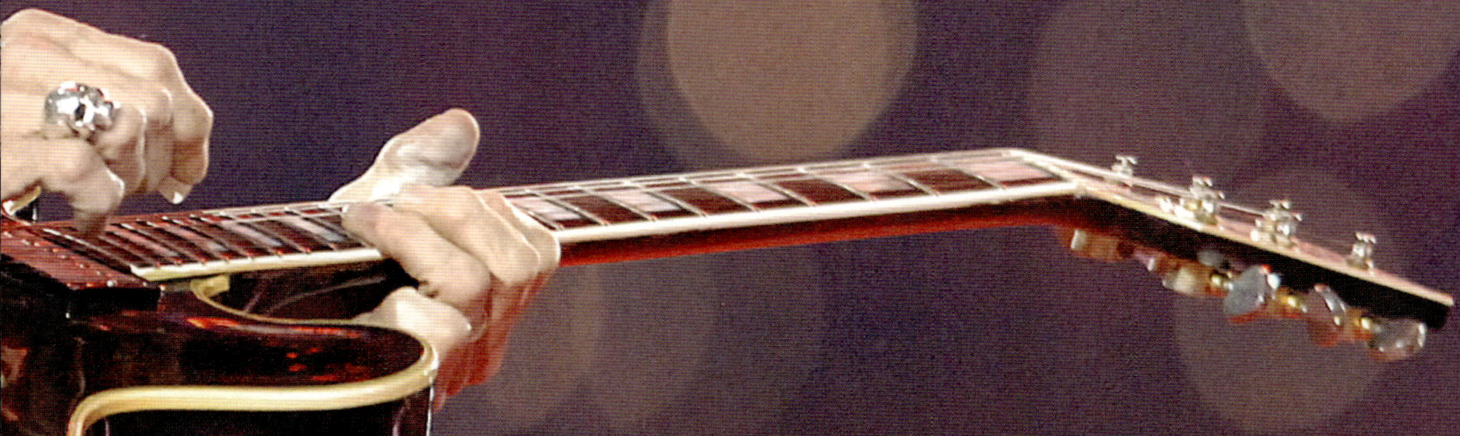

Jagger's destination when he ran into Keith on the station that fateful day half a century ago was the London School of Economics. It's no surprise, then, to find he is the business brain of the duo. He's also traditionally been the spokesperson for the group – but Keith has emerged from the shadows in recent years, particularly if he has had something to sell.

And it was publicity of his 2010 autobiography *Life* that appears to have driven the latest wedge between the Glimmer Twins. When in 2011 Mick was promoting his latest extra-curricular project, *Superheavy*, the 68-year-old strutted in a similar pink suit to the one in which he had promoted *Brown Sugar*, exactly four decades before. The difference was he did not have Keith Richards by his side. Whether a miracle reconciliation was on the cards remained to be seen, but all right-minded Stones fans had their fingers crossed.

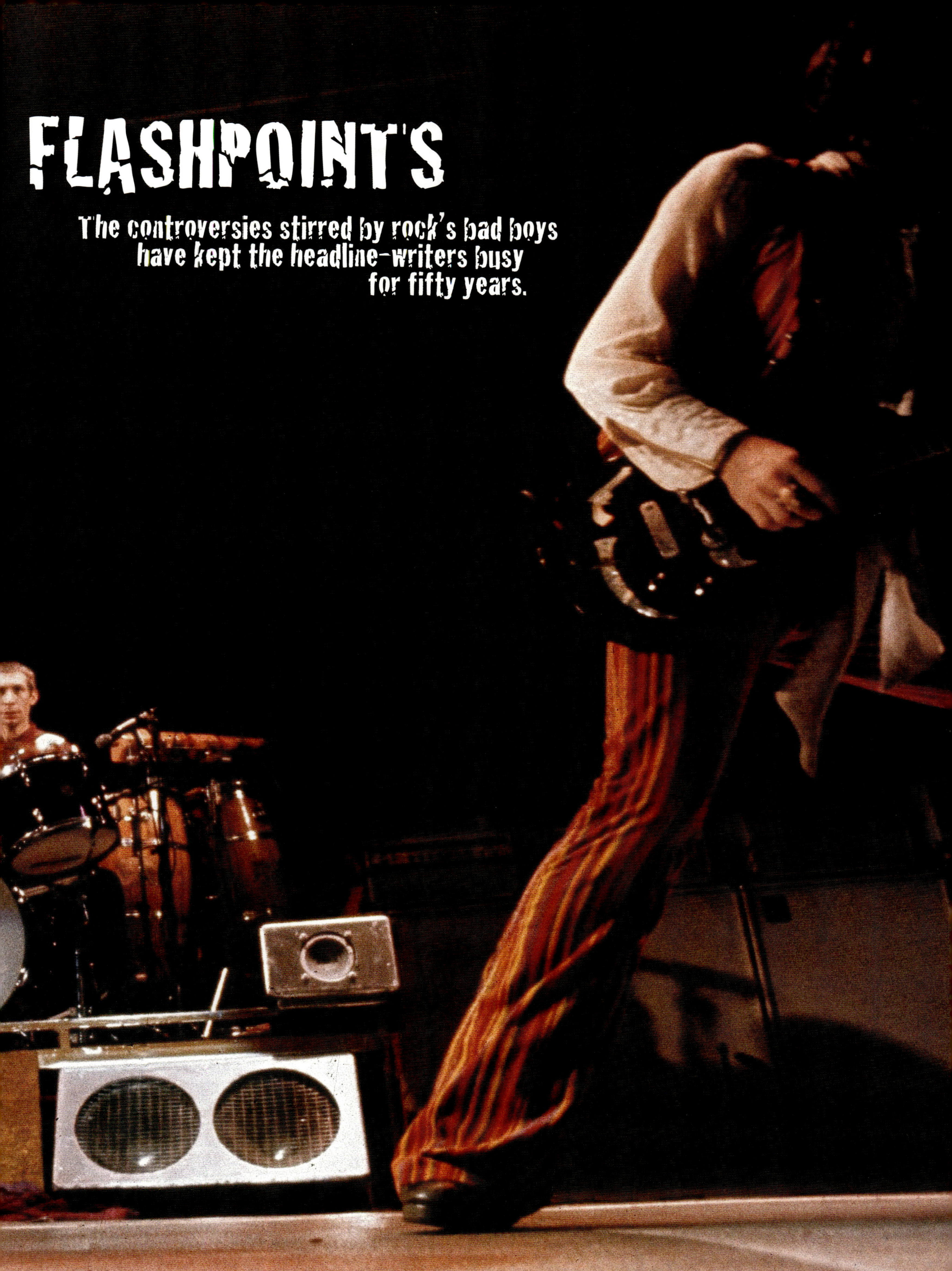

FLASHPOINT'S
The controversies stirred by rock's bad boys
have kept the headline-writers busy
for fifty years.

The Rolling Stones were always happy to play up (or down) to public expectations of their role as wild men of rock. A large part of that was down to Andrew Loog Oldham (left centre), the man who shared their early-Sixties management with Eric Easton. The older, more experienced Easton arranged tours while Oldham, barely out of his teens, used skills honed as a publicist with Brian Epstein to get the headlines.

On 18 March 1965, the same day *The Last Time* started its three-week reign at UK #1, three of the Stones – Wyman, Jagger and Jones – were caught using the wall of a London petrol station as a urinal. Bill Wyman had asked if he could go to the lavatory at the Francis Petrol Station in East Ham, but was refused. £5 fines all round resulted from the 'spent penny', Jagger having apparently declared: "We will piss anywhere, man."

Record releases always offered a good opportunity to cause a sensation. In October 1966 the group scandalised the British press by dressing in drag for publicity photos for the UK #5 hit *Have You Seen Your Mother, Baby*. Bill Wyman added fuel to the flames by being pictured in a wheelchair. A similar furore boiled up two years later when the original sleeve of the album *Beggars Banquet* showed a toilet wall covered in graffiti.

The year of 1967 had seen Mick and Keith spend a night apiece in jail before receiving bail. They had been charged following the February bust at Redlands, Keith's country house in Sussex. Their convictions on drug offences would be the subject of much debate in the press. Brian Jones, however, was in considerably deeper, his drugs convictions placing the Stones' ability to tour the States in jeopardy.

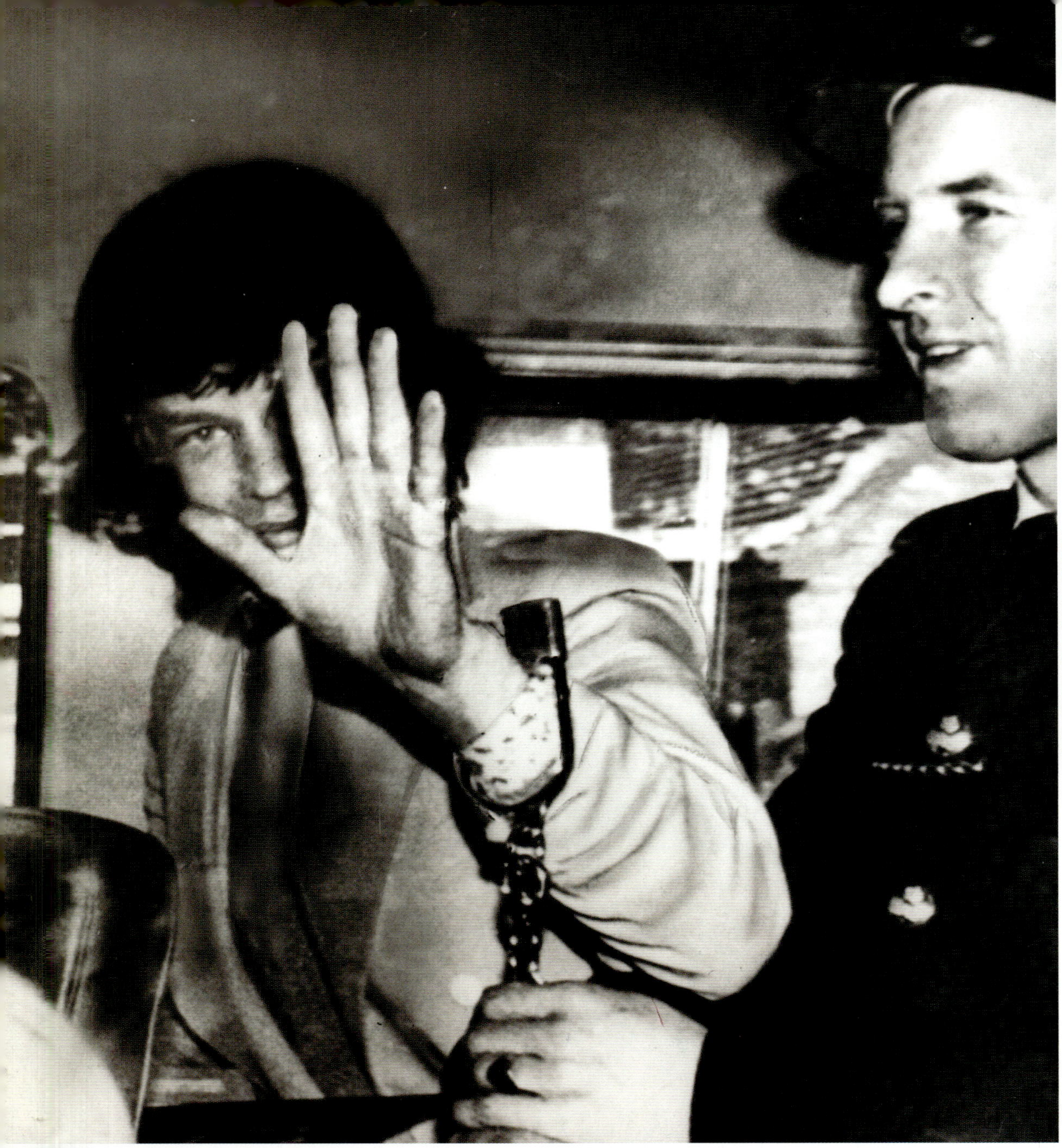

Sadly, Brian played less and less of a role in creating the music of the band he had played such a major part in forming, and he was found dead in the swimming pool of his house on 3 July 1969. Bill and Charlie attended his funeral, held a week later in his home town of Cheltenham.

The band's sixth US tour went ahead later that year with new guitarist Mick Taylor replacing Jones in the ranks. But a late date added at the Altamont speedway circuit in Northern California would mark the band's collective lowest point as an 18-year-old audience member, Meredith Hunter, was fatally stabbed during the Stones' performance. This was one headline the band would happily have done without.

Mick had been busted for drugs again in 1969 in the company of his then girlfriend Marianne Faithfull, but the Stones' decision to become tax exiles and base themselves in France removed

them from the long arm of the law – at least the British limb. But Keith did himself no favours when, in May 1976, he drove his Bentley into the central reservation of the M1 motorway in Buckinghamshire at 5am in the morning! Police had found cocaine and LSD in the limo.

Unfortunately for the human riff, his untidy habits would catch up with him again in February 1977, the month after the court case. His hotel room in Toronto was invaded by Mounties who seized quantities of substances suspected to be heroin and cocaine. Richards was released on probation.

The Eighties was quiet as domesticity finally kicked in. But evidence that the musical family was less than happy came in March 1986 as the album *Dirty Work* emerged. Mick later called it "a terrible period; everyone was hating each other so much. Everyone was so out of their brains, and Charlie was in seriously bad shape." Watts later confessed to substance abuse problems, leading to the use of a substitute drummer, while Jimmy Page, Bobby Womack and Tom Waits were among many musical guests used to paper over the cracks.

But the Stones continued rolling (with the occasional disagreement, as with Jagger's knighthood in 2003) until 2010. Keith's autobiography, serialised in *The Times* that October, took personal swipes at his band mate, such as "It was the beginning of the Eighties when Mick started to become unbearable." He revealed his nicknames for Jagger were 'Brenda' or 'Your Majesty', and likened living with Mick to coping with an annoying mynah bird.

Richards summarised the current distance between the pair by saying: "I used to love Mick, but I haven't been to his dressing room in 20 years. Sometimes I think, 'I miss my friend'. I wonder, 'Where did he go?'" These comments, plus remarks on the small size of Mick's manhood, drove a wedge between the pair that, sadly, continues today.

"I'm always shy in front of an audience,
so I'm always at the back, in the shadows, just
doing it. I don't like the front, the adulation."
Bill Wyman

It's Only Rock'n'Roll

A Rolling Stones Top 20 with chart honours and fascinating facts.

1. Angie (1973 – UK: 5 US: 1)

Fans and critics were falling over each other to guess the inspiration for *Angie* – David Bowie's wife Angela? *Ocean's Eleven* star Angie Dickinson? Keith Richards' newborn daughter Dandelion Angela? Regardless, it was a daring standalone ballad at a time when heavy rock ruled the roost.

2. Sympathy For The Devil (1968 – No Single Release)

Sung through the eyes of the devil himself and referencing the assassination of the Kennedy brothers, this was reported to be the song playing when concert-goer Meredith Hunter was fatally stabbed by a Hell's Angel at the Altamont free festival in 1969. It was in fact the last lines of *Under My Thumb*, but the song retains its ability to chill.

3. Gimme Shelter (1969 – No Single Release)

Never released as a single, the impassioned opener to 1969's *Let It Bleed* album quickly became a cult classic among fans. It cemented its place as a staple of the Stones' shows and even charted at #38 in Rolling Stone's 500 Greatest Songs of All Time, despite never hitting the singles listings.

4. Midnight Rambler (1969 – No Single Release)

Another Stones classic never to be released on 45, *Midnight Rambler* is a disturbing tale reportedly inspired by the Boston Strangler murders of 1962-64. It was again the performance of the track on stage that sparked its popularity, energetic and often disturbing performances often stretching beyond ten minutes.

5. (I Can't Get No) Satisfaction (1965 – UK: 1 US: 1)

Perhaps the Stones' most instantly recognisable track, appearing on many magazines' top songs of all time charts. The riff came to Keith Richards in his sleep and was captured on a tape recorder handily situated next to his hotel-room bed. The fuzzed guitar notes were supposed to be horns, and Otis Redding's version of the song is truer to his original concept.

6. Ruby Tuesday (1967 – UK: 3 US: 1)

The hallmark of the Jagger/Richards songwriting duo was imprinted on almost all the Rolling Stones tracks, but there are suggestions that that another bandmate had a hand in crafting this US #1 hit. Marianne Faithfull claims that the late Brian Jones created the original melody, though his name never appeared on the credits.

7. Anybody Seen My Baby (1997 – UK: 22 US: -)

When Jagger and Richards discovered that the chorus of their 1997 track sounded almost exactly like that of Canadian country singer kd lang's 1992 hit *Constant Craving*, they gave her and songwriting partner Ben Mink credit just to avoid any post-release complications.

8. Paint It Black (1966 – UK: 1 US: 1)

Paint It Black features the sitar played by Brian Jones. The inclusion of the Indian stringed instrument is owed to a member of another world-famous British band – Beatle George Harrison. The extravagantly talented Jones picked up the instrument after visiting Harrison who, at the time, was discovering Eastern culture. He taught himself to play, and the result was the icing on a transatlantic chart-topper.

9. Under My Thumb (1966 – No Single Release)

By reversing a well-used phrase, Jagger managed to cause controversy and enrage the growing feminist movement. After denying for years that the track was denigrating women in any way, Jagger snapped in 1984, saying: "The whole idea was that I was under her – she was kicking me around. The whole idea is absurd; all I did was turn the tables around."

10. Wild Horses (1971 – UK: – US: 28)

This single's cover was the first to feature the Stones' iconic tongue logo, designed by John Pasche. As he recalls, the inspiration was none other than Jagger himself; other sources suggest the Indian god Kali. The song was originally given to Gram Parsons of the Flying Burrito Brothers, hence its easy-paced country ballad style.

11. Start Me Up (1981 – UK: 7 US: 2)

After enjoying success upon its 1981 release, *Start Me Up* would become synonymous with the start of a revolution more than a decade later when Microsoft paid a reported $3 million to use the track as the theme for its Windows 95 computer operating system.

12. Brown Sugar (1971 – UK: 2 US: 1)

Brown Sugar was considered risqué in 1971, with talk of heroin and interracial sex as the track's possible inspirations. But fast-forward into the twenty first century and the song was still drawing ire from some corners of the world – namely China. The country's authorities requested that the band didn't play the track during a Shanghai gig.

13. Honky Tonk Women (1969 – UK: 1 US: 1)

Honky Tonk Women signals another foray into the world of country music for the Stones, with the inclusion of producer Jimmy Miller on cowbell; the band even recorded a full-on country version titled *Country Honk*. But all this is slightly strange when you consider Jagger and Richards penned the track while soaking up the Latin culture of Brazil!

14. The Last Time (1965 – UK: 1 US: 9)

The Last Time holds a special significance for the Stones; it is the first track penned by the now-legendary songwriting partnership of Mick Jagger and Keith Richards to hit UK #1. The track toppled Welsh balladeer Tom Jones from the top spot in their home country.

15. It's Only Rock'n'Roll (1974 – UK: 10 US: 16)

After more than a decade on the stage and in the public eye, the Stones found themselves in the Seventies on the receiving end from some critics. Jagger and Richards penned this tongue-in-cheek response to silence their detractors. "I was getting a bit tired of that, 'Oh, it's not as good as their last one' business," said Jagger.

16. Miss You (1978 – UK: 3 US: 1)

The Stones go disco, and make a good fist of it for their eighth and last US chart-topping single. Charlie Watts said his contribution to the song was heavily influenced by "those four-to-the-floor and the Philadelphia-style drumming", while Bill Wyman's octave bass lines were very much of the moment. Yet the song had been cooked up by Mick Jagger and Billy Preston the previous year when rehearsing for the Toronto club gigs.

17. Street Fighting Man (1968 – UK: 21 US: 48)

Designed to cash in on the political unrest over Vietnam, Jagger wrote *Street Fighting Man* after attending a London anti-war rally in early 1968. The song was predictably banned by US radio, only reaching #48 as a consequence. The single did not see a release in the United Kingdom until 1971, and is unlikely to be performed live again.

18. Jumpin' Jack Flash (1968 – UK: 1 US: 3)

Jumpin' Jack Flash gave the band their first UK #1 single for nearly two years in June 1968. Much covered by Johnny Winter, Peter Frampton, Tina Turner and many others, this was released barely a month after being recorded at Olympic Studios in London and was not to appear on the later album *Beggars Banquet*. It's been played on every Stones tour since its release; the Jack of the title is Keith's gardener.

19. Fool To Cry (1976 – UK: 6 US: 10)

Another sublime Stones slowie to offset the rockers, this rivals *Angie* as the decade's best ballad and brought the soulful best out of Jagger's voice. Released as the lead single off *Black And Blue* in April 1976, it quickly found its way into the band's set, and a video was shot in Kiel, Germany, to promote it to transatlantic Top 10 status.

20. Let's Spend The Night Together (1967 – UK: 3 US: 55)

Let's Spend The Night Together kicked off the Stones' worst year, 1967, when it was released in January. It was censored by US television, Jagger agreeing to sing *Let's Spend Some Time Together* while rolling his eyes insolently. The insistent piano on the original was played jointly by Keith and American record producer Jack Nitzsche.

STONES TIMELINE

24 October, 1936 - Bill Wyman is born.

2 June, 1941 - Charlie Watts is born.

28 February, 1942 - Brian Jones is born.

1943

26 July - Mick Jagger is born.

18 December - Keith Richards is born.

1 June, 1947 - Ron Wood is born.

17 January, 1949 - Mick Taylor is born

1960

Keith Richards and Mick Jagger meet on Dartford station.

1962

12 July - The embryonic Stones featuring Mick, Keith and Brian play London's Marquee Club.

15 December - Bill Wyman plays his first Stones gig at Putney Church Hall.

1963

January - Charlie Watts' first gig at Soho's Flamingo Jazz Club.

24 February - First date of a Sunday-night residency at the Station Hotel, Richmond.

7 June - First single, *Come On*, is released by Decca Records.

1964

2 May – Debut album *Rolling Stones* reaches UK Number 1.

5 June - The Stones' first US tour opens at San Bernardino as *It's All Over Now* becomes their first Number 1 single in the UK.

1965

21 January - First Australasian/Far East tour.

6 February – *Rolling Stones No 2* tops the UK album chart.

24 September – *Out Of Our Heads* is kept off UK Number 1 by *The Sound of Music* soundtrack.

1966

19 February - *19th Nervous Breakdown* ends a run of five successive UK Number 1 singles by peaking at Number 2.

April - *Aftermath* spends the first of eight weeks at UK Number 1.

1967

5 February - *Between The Buttons* heads for UK Number 3 as the Stones sue the *News Of The World* newspaper.

12 February - Redlands, Keith's country house, is raided by police. Mick and Keith spend a night in jail in June on drugs charges.

29 September - The Stones and manager Andrew Oldham part company.

1968

January – The Stones' 'psychedelic' album *Their Satanic Majesties Request* reaches UK Number 3/US Number 2.

June - *Jumpin' Jack Flash* is the band's first UK Number 1 single for almost two years.

5 December – *Beggar's Banquet*, a UK Number 3 album, appears in a censored white sleeve.

11-12 December - The Lennons, Eric Clapton, Jethro Tull, Marianne Faithfull and the Who join the Stones for the Rock And Roll Circus TV special.

1969

13 June - Mick Taylor replaces Brian Jones as lead guitarist.

3 July - Brian is found dead in the swimming pool of his house.

5 July - The Stones play Hyde Park, dedicating the day to Brian.

6 December - A date at the Altamont speedway circuit in California sees audience member Meredith Hunter fatally stabbed by a member of the Hell's Angels.

20 December – Last Decca studio LP *Let It Bleed* reaches UK Number 1.

1970

1 August – Premiere of *Performance*, a movie starring Mick Jagger and Anita Pallenberg.

1971

May – Transatlantic chart-topper *Sticky Fingers*, containing the classic *Brown Sugar*, is the first album released on Rolling Stones Records.

12 May - Mick marries Bianca Perez Moreno de Macias. Daughter Jade is born on 21 October.

1972

26 May - Double vinyl album *Exile On Main Street* heralds a two-month North American tour.

1973

31 July - Redlands is damaged by fire but Keith, who escapes unhurt, has it rebuilt.

September - The band tours Britain and Germany as *Goat's Head Soup* heads for UK/US Number 1. Contains the hit single *Angie*.

1974

October – *It's Only Rock 'n' roll*, with production by Mick and Keith, tops the US chart.

12 December - Mick Taylor quits the band.

1975

14 April - Ron Wood is named fifth Stone for a US tour that opens in Louisiana in June.

1976

April – *Black And Blue* moves to Number 2 in the UK charts (US Number 1).

June - Keith and Anita's son Tara dies in a Geneva hospital, aged ten weeks.

21 August - The Stones play to 200,000 at Knebworth House, Hertfordshire.

1977

12 January - Keith is found guilty of possessing cocaine.

24 February - Keith and partner Anita Pallenberg are stopped at Toronto Airport and Anita's bags are searched. She is charged with possession of cannabis and heroin, while Keith is charged later that week for possession with intent to sell.

4-5 March - The band plays to an audience of 300 at Toronto's El Mocambo Club for future album *Love You Live*.

1978

10 June - The album *Some Girls* and single *Miss You* head for the top of the US chart as the band start a ninth Stateside tour.

1979

2 November – Mick and Bianca Perez Moreno de Macias divorce.

1980

April – *Emotional Rescue* tops both the UK and US charts.

July - Keith and Anita separate.

1981

September – *Tattoo You* tops the US charts, makes Number 2 in Britain and contains a big hit single in *Start Me Up*.

1982

June – *Still Life*, recorded on the previous year's US tour, is released as the band tour Europe.

1983

November – *Undercover* causes controversy for the violent content of its title track's video.

December - Keith marries Patti Hansen on his 40th birthday.